# ONLY IN AMERICA

ALEX OSBORNE

Only in America
First Printing: 2013

ISBN: 978-0989363617



Pseudo Poseur Productions
116 W. 12th St.
Wayne, Ne 68787
America

pseudoposeur.com

Journalism



Editors: Alex Osborne, Kacey Caffoor and Chad M. Christensen
Copy Editors: Kayla Lucht and WSC Editing for Publications Class
Cover Design: Rory Gove
Front Cover Photo: Chad Christensen
Back Cover Photo: Rory Gove
Background Photo: Kate Elrington
Book Design: Pseudo Poseur

The publisher and the editors would like to thank *The Wayne Stater* and *Nebby* for permission to reprint the following works.

Dedicated to everyone who stuck by me while I went on this adventure, and recommended to anyone who hit the piss with me on a regular basis.

# Contents

## Foreword



## Columns

## Guest Columns



## Final Thoughts



## Glossary

# Foreword:
## Sex, Drugs and Rock 'N' Roll

Alex Osborne is not only an astute and candid writer and a close friend, but also my polar opposite. Our views could not be any more contrasting, and this has, somehow, created our bond.

I am a typical farm boy, while Alex is an Australian city kid from Melbourne; our history initially set us apart. Other differences include: politics – Conservative vs. Liberal; religion – Christian vs. Jedi; and leanings – artistic vs. athletic, setting the stage for two individuals destined, practically guaranteed, to never cross paths.

A shared college campus, our escapades on it, and the stars aligning, set not only the scene for our meeting but also the frame for this collection of work.

There is nothing off-limits in the pages that you are about to read. Love and hatred collide in tales of confusion and understanding. Many end with more questions than they began with, but the fact that you are asking yourself these questions is what is important.

Alex makes his points with authentic Aussie flair and an undeniable sense of humor. Although the Land Down Under shares more than a handful of traits with my homeland in the U.S. of A, language is apparently not one of them.

It seems that English is less than universal across the nations. Buff up on your Aussie lingo, as the language barrier is no laughing matter. 'Jugs,' 'bins,' 'jumpers' and 'root' translate to 'pitchers,' 'trashcans,' 'sweatshirts' and 'crazed sexual encounter.' Throw a few words into Google and flip through the Glossary to fill in any blanks.

It is my pleasure to introduce this book to you. I guarantee that the time you spend between these pages with Alex will be as entertaining as every night he and I spent together tearing up the town.

One love,
Matt Richardson
News Editor for *The Wayne Stater*

"'Only in America.' Say this when you find something different and maybe annoying. It will help you cope with the differences in culture and practice."

Adrienne Osborne
My Mum

# IT'S A PIZZA?

*Published in* The Wayne Stater *31/08/2011*

It had come to my attention that the life of a columnist like Kevin Smith (also a movie and comic writer), would be a much easier and more comedic one than that of a beat reporter – no interviews and such. Then, however, was the unforeseen difficulty of thinking of something to write about. Interviewing a football player seems to be an easier option right now.

So while killing time checking Facebook for the sixth time this hour, I receive a chat message from one of my best mates, Rick "11:30 Rick" Crichton. I start telling him a story or two, both of which end with us saying, "Only in America." Then it hits me: every day I see something that happens here in the United States that doesn't happen back home in Australia.

A couple of days ago I went to Pizza Hut for lunch, because – let's face it – no matter who you are, you like pizza and wings. I usually end up picking the simple toppings like pepperoni because they have deals on one-topping pizzas. This time, however, I decide to splurge and go for something I have never had before.

I order the "El Rancho" pizza. I understand this to mean "The Ranch" pizza in English. The pizza consists of chicken and ranch dressing as the main toppings. Once it is out of the oven, fresh lettuce, tomatoes and onions are added, turning what I thought was going to be a pizza into some sort of chicken salad on pizza dough.

"Only in America," I suppose; fairly different compared to the "Aussie" pizza (ham, egg, bacon and onion) or – what I usually order – the Capricciosa (ham, mushrooms, olives and anchovies) or the Deluxe Supreme.

Anyway, to avoid this turning into a rant about pizza toppings, I will get to my point. I can't eat all of the pizza because I filled up on the good stuff – spicy BBQ wings. So I take the rest home; another foreign concept.

In Australia, people can usually finish their orders. Meal portion sizes in America are massive; but that's another topic.

I decide to reheat it later. Then I run into the predicament of how to reheat, since microwaved lettuce isn't on my agenda.

What do I do? If someone has a better suggestion than what I am about to unravel, please approach me in the playground, but keep in mind, I prefer warm pizza to cold pizza.

I end up scraping all the lettuce and tomato off with a knife, however, there is a layer stuck to the melted cheese. This takes three minutes to get off. After another three minutes of reheating, I spend two minutes re-adding the topping. If you're not a mathematician that's eight minutes; way too long for left-over pizza.

What I got out of this experience was this: do not mess with what works. Pizza is not supposed to have lettuce on it, and only in America does it.

The El Rancho pizza

# AMERICA HATES THE BLIND

*Published in* Nebby *in Issue 22 19/10/2011*

Apparently I stumbled onto a good idea: a certain someone told me, "I like the theme, but tell me what you really think; *Nebby* isn't worried about offending its readership."

Something along those lines at least. I forget his name, I think it was Charlie, or maybe that's just what he was on. It went from a light entertainment idea (which involved selling out to the masses) to an "Oi! This is what I'd tell me mate back home." So 'ere goes…

I am sitting in the pub, a common occurrence for a journalism major. We have a lot of down time, with very little up time.

I order another pot and start fumbling with my wallet to pay my tab. Every note in my wallet is the same size and colour and I am too blind-drunk to read the numbers in the corners. Australian money comes in different colours and different sizes, with different clear windows of braille – all which help in this situation.

Speaking of braille, I was at a drive-thru ATM and the numbers on the keypad had braille on them, yet the buttons on the side, where you select 'withdraw' or whatever, did not.

Even the ATM cannot tell the difference in the money and only bloody disperses me 20s. I'm withdrawing a couple hundred at a time, so my wallet is fat to say the least (later this month the note pocket rips under pressure). I hand the bartender what I hope is two 20s – she hands me the change – I can't see what she is handing me, so I guess and slap down what is possibly a poor excuse for a tip.

Now, my flat is only a cooee from the bar, but I walk to the pedestrian lights because I'm too smashed to trust my eyes. I push the button and am leaning on the pole for support for what seems like five minutes. "Why hasn't the light changed?" I wonder. Well that's because it has changed and in America there is not an audible cue for we, the blind. There is, however, a visible cue telling me I have five seconds to cross a four-lane highway. Fark!

This whole experience really has me thinking about the life of a blind person. Not a frequent visitor like I might be: I am talking about a person you would go out of your way to help (well, at least I'd hope so). Life for them really isn't fair. America's public transport system sucks so bad they would need a little extra help to get around.

The expression "the blind leading the blind" has real life

application when it comes to the American government it is incapable of getting around without help from its over-aggressive nuclear presence, and is getting around wherever it wants because of it, leading its incapable citizens along.

It is clear that only in America do they hate the blind because they themselves are blind.

# HAMBURGERS

When you think of hamburgers, what do you think of? I'm guessing something along the lines of Macca's or Hungry Jack's, or learning German and realising the only phrase you remember is "das ist mein hamburger." Well, for me, I think of Americans, and how that is all they seem to eat.

At the time of this writing, I work as Lunch Lady Doris; my job is to make hamburgers for rude Americans who go to Wayne State College. I do this three days a week, the other two I am a dishy. I prefer lunch lady – more to look at, if you catch my drift.

Student after student comes up to order a hamburger. What I do is put a burger patty in a bun, then slide it down to the guy, who always talks about how much he doesn't talk, who gives them their hot chips. Before the plate has finished sliding, I cop the Lily Aldrin "you're dead to me look," because apparently I forgot the cheese. I politely remind them, that they should have ordered a cheeseburger if they wanted cheese.

If you go to Macca's and order a hamburger, guess what? No cheese.

So now, I have to ask them which cheese they would like. I usually get "American" snapped back at me, as if I had asked what nationality they were.

The hamburger was apparently invented in Texas in 1880; the cheeseburger, mind you, not invented until 1925 in California. So the facts are clear. It's not because I am Australian – there is an obvious difference between a hamburger and a cheeseburger.

Maybe next time you're in McDonald's and they bugger up your order, contemplate these thoughts.

Only in America can they invent the hamburger and still order it wrong.

# WORLDWIDE AMERICAN HOLIDAY

Do Americans celebrate Melbourne Cup Day, ANZAC Day, the Queen's Birthday, Labour Day (with a U), or Australia Day?

Of course not. So imagine asking that same question but substituting in American holidays. For example, the one that's just around the corner, Thanksgiving.

To my surprise during this past week, when asking people what they were going to do with their five days off school for Thanksgiving, the answers I received were along the lines of: "not much, eat a ton of food, watch football, and do you celebrate Thanksgiving in Australia?"

Correct me if I am wrong here, but isn't Thanksgiving for celebrating the time when the Native Americans helped the Pilgrims survive their first winters in America in the 1600s?

So I turned the question back onto them. "Do you even know the meaning of Thanksgiving?" Not one person out of an approximate ten withdrew their original question.

"Doesn't, like, everyone else in the world want to be like America? So, like, why wouldn't they, like, celebrate it?" one person said. Obviously a blonde girl who has never left Nebraska in her life, or as my mate Jewels would say, "a valley girl."

Another said, "everyone celebrates St. Patrick's Day, I just assumed Thanksgiving was the same." He got me with that response.

About five or six of the people who asked, legitimately did not know the meaning of Thanksgiving, so they couldn't comprehend why it was a dumb question. Also because their teachers told them growing up that there was no such thing as a dumb question. If you have ever read "Ask a Foreigner" on my entertainment page, then you know very well that there is.

It blew my mind to hear these comments, especially on a holiday that quite frankly, I could get down with. A couple days off school to eat a lot of food and drink beer – who could turn that down?

Only in America are American holidays celebrated worldwide, but other countries' traditions neglected. For example, not letting me play the Australian National Anthem on Australia Day before a basketball game.

# RELIGION IS NO JOKE

A couple of weeks ago, the (probably) now infamous Kayla Clark wrote a piece on copping a little criticism from a religious group here at Wayne State College. Whether I was included in her "fourth floor family" or not, it is in the past and I forgive her, which seems like a hard thing for religious groups to do.

In America, God seems to be everything. 'God Bless America'; 'In God We Trust.' Before you say, "But you have *God Save the Queen*," let me remind you that I am Australian, and in 1984, *God Save the Queen* was voted out as our national anthem and *Advance Australia Fair* was chosen in its place. There was a Christian movement to add a second verse, however our prime minister said, "under national protocols, the anthem should not be modified."

I'm not trying to say I don't believe in or respect the Christian image of God. It is just that I don't believe I have to answer to a higher power outside of my mum's house.

Whether this means I am cremated and smoked for my knowledge like in *How High*, or I have the privilege of going to that place in the sky with my boy Obi Wan Kenobi – yes, a *Star Wars* reference, there's more – I am not fussed.

In 2001, what is known as the Jedi Census Phenomenon occurred for the first time in many English speaking countries, except, of course, America. The Jedi Census Phenomenon is when people answer Jedi, Jedi Knight or Jediism to the religion question on national censuses.

Australia's total was 70,000. There could have been many reasons why people answered Jedi, whether it was because *Star Wars* is awesome, to take the piss out of religion, or to upset the government. I would presume that it was a protest to the question having any relevance in today's society.

I went to a religious high school for one year, and it was one year too many. My religious education teacher asked that I be excused from his class for my highly opinionated comments. I could sit here all day and argue any and all religious beliefs with you. But if you make it day-to-day and you're all sweet, then who cares if "God" was the inventor of the world's first clap-on light or if it was Mr. Joseph Enterprises. All I know, is that me and the Christian news editor will still be grabbing a beer long into the night, regardless of whether he believes I am a Jedi Knight or not.

It is a joke to think that religion matters in today's society, and of English speaking countries, only in America is it taken so seriously.

# THE MOST DEPRESSING TIME OF THE YEAR

*Published in* The Wayne Stater *30/11/2011*

To many, Christmas is the most wonderful time of the year, and the Christmas song says it all.

However, to an Australian spending his fourth Christmas in Nebraska, it becomes an extremely depressing time.

In Australia, Christmas is a summer holiday: three or four months off school, beaches, BBQs and music festivals. Compared to Nebraska – two or three weeks off school, snowed in at your girlfriend's mum's house with a kitchen you can't use because cooking creates mess.

My first winter in America was the first time I saw snow, and it was as exciting as can be. I made snowmen and snow angels, had a snowball fight, played tiggy on a frozen-over billabong and used a bin lid to slide down the hill to get to basketball practice. But then that week passed and I was just cold, for the rest of the school year.

Snow is horrible, and the ideal white Christmas is just impractical.

In 2009 I thought I would finally get to spend Christmas with a family and experience everything a Nebraskan Christmas has to offer, hopefully making it the fabled most wonderful time of the year.

Mate, was I wrong. I spent a good two or three hours shovelling snow out of the driveway and the street just so we could get the car out. Once the car was out and we'd had lunch, I spent another hour getting out of *that* driveway, just so we could get stuck in our street and have to push the car home.

Christmas 2010 was a different story – I was back in Melbourne. The weather was nice and I had Christmas lunch outside with my family at a friend's house. To reinforce a little stereotype, I even saw a kangaroo along the way, albeit dead in the gutter.

For lunch, we had king prawns and lobsters. That night, I went and sat poolside at a mate's place, drinking Crown Lager which I won in a bet.

Which sounds like the better Christmas?

To make matters worse, back in the U.S., I was stuck inside with people asking me if there is Christmas in Australia. Not as bad as asking if we celebrate Thanksgiving, but still very annoying.

We do celebrate Christmas, but only at Christmas time. Our

Santa Claus is not the Coca-Cola image of Santa, because that Santa would have a heat stroke coming to my house.

We even changed the Jingle Bells song.

"Dashing through the bush,
In a rusty Holden Ute,
Kicking up the dust,
Esky in the boot,
Kelpie by my side,
Singing Christmas songs,
It's summer time and I am in
My singlet, shorts and thongs."

So, yes, our Santa drives a Holden Ute and wears a singlet, shorts and thongs and has plenty of stubbies in the Esky.

In my letter to Santa this year, I was quite blunt and to the point.

"Dear Santa, don't f*** with me this year, and please ask Chartwells to pay me a decent wage so I can buy the new Call of Duty already. Catch maaate."

So the next time you're singing a little Andy Williams, remember – in America, Christmas is the most depressing time of the year.

Christmas 2009, Nebraska

# FOOTBALL ABOVE ALL

with Matt Richardson (News Editor at *The Wayne Stater*)

*Published in* The Wayne Stater *16/11/2011*

Last week something was finally done to stop a priest from touching little boys at a church in Pennsylvania. It became apparent that the bishop knew about the alleged sexual assaults on 10-year-old altar boys from the priest under his supervision.

While the Catholic Church continues to cop scrutiny in the press for covering up sexual assaults, the church in question here is one worshipped by the entire nation.

College football.

Students took to the streets, turning over a news van in a demonstration that made the VEISHA riots at Iowa State University seem like the PRIDE Parade.

Were the riots due to outrage over the alleged acts? Were they in support of the victims and their families? Or was it because it was 10 p.m., and they were looking for an excuse to get rowdy like Roddy Piper?

Such questions arose last Wednesday over how college football's 'winningest' coach could be fired over a situation that was 15 years old. Opinions concerning how much responsibility can be pinned on the coach Joe Paterno are varied.

As an employee of any school, you must first report issues to your superiors. There is a chain of command that must be followed. It is protocol and it is mandatory.

But what if further action needs to be taken?

Is it then the coach's responsibility to take that action? Is it the person who witnessed the incident? Is it perhaps the athletic director or even the school president?

Although these allegations have only recently gained national and worldwide attention, the proposed instances didn't just happen yesterday. These issues are well over a decade old. Who are these victims? Where have these victims been for the past 15 years? We know that they are obviously males and now land somewhere in their 20s.

So why is this an issue now? These acts are clearly unforgivable and an absolute tragedy, but when assigning blame, where does it stop?

How is it that thousands of students take to the streets in support of the head of their "church," who was fired for not doing enough to stop alleged sexual assaults on adolescent boys? Only in America does football hold such prominence.

Only in America is football above all.

# 20 PAGES IN 12 HOURS

with Matt Richardson (News Editor at *The Wayne Stater*)

*Published in* The Wayne Stater *02/11/2011*

*The Wayne Stater* is put together each week by a group of dedicated and hard-working student editors.

These students are assigned the task of selecting the most newsworthy stories, placing them with their respective photos, creating effective headlines and editing stories for accuracy.

The majority of this work is done on Tuesday over the course of roughly 12 hours, beginning early in the day and ending in the wee hours of Wednesday morning.

Although it is no simple task, we, as student editors, take part in this opportunity because we like it, and we take pride in what we do.

This is why we have chosen to further our education at Wayne State College, to be a part of a full-bodied weekly publication that will prepare us for finding a career in the journalism field upon graduation.

This is what we want to do, and as with any task, perfection is difficult to obtain.

We do not make excuses for our mistakes, but rather own up to them and print corrections in the next issue. At times, these mistakes offend readers, but it is not our intention to do so.

We are students just trying to learn the trade, gain experience, and grow from our successes and failures. Criticism is part of any working atmosphere.

Mistakes will occur in any environment, and it is learning from these that will ultimately help you become better at what you do.

The key to this cycle is keeping the criticism constructive with the overall improvement of the individual project at heart.

Many *Stater* staff writers are freshmen and sophomore journalism majors submitting their first published works, with the editors having an additional year or two of experience combined with the burden of significantly multiplied responsibilities.

*The Wayne Stater* is a student-run, student-contributed newspaper for us to gain the necessary experience to move on after college.

The motive behind our responsibility as editors is far from financial; quite the opposite at our towering $1.48 per hour salary. It's tough to complain about this situation as the copy editors that spend their hours hunched over countless articles with red ink pens in hand do it simply for course credit and the good of the publication.

If you disagree with what we are doing, don't hide behind a letter or e-mail.

If we are not living up to your standards, perhaps you can do better? Maybe there are too many mistakes? Maybe you're just unhappy with our performance?

If you think we are sending a terrible message about our writers, our paper or Wayne State College, we are looking forward to seeing you on Tuesday nights.

Only in America are you called an *amature* for being an amateur.

# DON'T FORGET TO PAY SHIPPING AND HANDLING

Picture this: last call comes around and you don't have enough cash to buy that last drink. You whip out your card and as you are signing off on the purchase you read the word "tip," and all of a sudden you realise where your money went.

The whole night you thought the pretty bartender was actually interested in your life. When really she was just trying to suck that extra dollar out of you, not suck anything else.

When you order something online, usually you have to pay some sort of shipping and handling fee. Basically, paying a deliveryman to go from the warehouse to your house with whatever it might be.

Now, this job consists of delivering packages as they are requested. He might say, "g'day", but then he buggers off. Apply this concept to bartenders. You say, "G'day, chuck us a pint'a" – you know, whatever – "Coors". The bartender's job is to go to the tap, pour the beer, and bring it back to you. There is a striking similarity between the two jobs.

The difference is, you have already paid the shipping and handling for the deliveryman who actually drives from a place that wasn't two steps away. The bartender takes a few steps, pours the beer and returns expecting compensation for her efforts. You don't have to tip but if you want repeated mediocre service, you kind of do. They will make small talk, large talk and you-think-you're-getting-somewhere talk, but it's not genuine.

I have noticed the mentality of men in bars; everyone wants to take the bartender home. I get it. I mean, I was engaged to one (however, I met her outside the bar scene).

Their preferred method for picking up the bartenders is to flash their cash. Almost as if throwing money at these girls will have them get naked – remind you of another profession? Throwing money at a girl only gets her clothes off at a strip club and no matter how much money you throw at them, even they aren't going to put out, because that only applies to prostitutes.

My main thought on tipping is, why is it up to society to pay bartenders to pour beer? Most people don't even order tap beer, now that I think about it. So why is it upon society to pay bartenders to get a beer from the fridge and open it? I am a poor college student, living in a college town, where all the bartenders are my classmates, who earn more money than I do, even without tips. It shouldn't fall on the broke college student to pay the less-broke college student.

Only in America does beer at the pub not include free shipping and handling.

## UGGS AND TWITTER

*Published in* The Wayne Stater *28/09/2011*

Recently, I have been battling a cold. The fact that it was freezing two weeks ago, then nice and warm last week, really messed with my body.

When I say it was freezing, I think I might have been the only one who was cold.

It got down to about 7 degrees Celsius – for those playing at home that's 45°Fahrenheit. The coldest it ever gets where I live in Melbourne is about 0°C (32°F), which is an overnight temperature. So as you can see, it's close to as cold as it gets for me.

Last Thursday was about 15°C (60°F) with, of course, a cold Nebraskan wind. I was rugged up for the worst: hat, jumper with hood, skivvy, trackies, and of course, my Ugg boots.

Now, I got teased a little bit at my last school for rocking my Uggs, but quite frankly, it was cold outside and they kept my extra-large feet warmer than runners.

I was sitting in Max's class, copy editing some news stories, when my phone went off. It was my news editor Matt asking if I was "rockin' the sweats and Uggs today?"

I replied, "Yeah! Crazy. Where'd you see me? I'm a little under the weather, just stayin' warm."

Matt replied, "HAHA! Guy tweeted about it! Lol! Not something people are used to seein' in Nebraska."

I flat-out refuse to use Twitter; I don't see the point of telling people every little thing that I am doing. "Jus' ate lol," "Grlz in my class are like sooo annoying."

In fact, I can't even pretend to mimic these "Tweets," because I can't bring myself to butcher the English language that much. However, when it came to some random guy tweeting about me, I had to check it out.

Matt sent me the screenshots. I was fascinated as to how this happened.

'Andyjay9' said, "Just saw a dude walking around campus wearing ugz with his sweats tucked in #whatisgoingon."

I actually remember walking past this bloke on the way into school.

There were a couple of replies to this, one from a good drinking partner (well, 'good' so long as she had no other blokes to get free drinks off), who shall remain anonymous to keep the authenticity of the drinking game I made up from watching her get free drinks all night. She said, "What do you expect, it's

Wayne, America."

The other was from Matt, who promptly assured the Twitter community that it was me.

This was about the extent of the 15 seconds of fame I received.

Imagine if I Tweeted every time I saw someone wearing cowboy boots or every time someone asked if I rode kangaroos. I'll tell you what; my hands would run more of a risk of developing carpal tunnel syndrome than on double XP weekends.

Only in America do you get Tweeted about for wearing Uggs.

# AMERICAN BEER

I recently watched a documentary on beer and how it saved the world. Throughout the doco it gave little snippets of what was to come after the break, and continuously mentioned that 'a country' was founded on beer. Eventually they got to the subject: it was, surprisingly, America.

The doco made me love beer even more, something I never thought possible. If beer founded America, how could it go wrong? I figured what better place to drink beer, than a place founded *on* beer.

After spending three years drinking light beer, I have developed an appreciation for good beer and have become quite the connoisseur.

I joined the World Beer Tour at the Old Chicago pub – attempting to drink 110 beers from around the world with prizes for milestones. I think it might be one of the only places in America where trying different beers is encouraged. The local bottle-o here in Wayne has a couple of different six-packs to offer, but nothing that is worth it when kicking in an extra $10 gets you a slab of the cheap stuff.

In Australia, light beer means low alcohol content. In America, it means low calorie. I did a little research on one of the domestic beers of choice in Australia, Victoria Bitter: it contains 146 calories and 4.9% alcohol. Some of the domestic choices in America include Bud Light, containing 110 calories and 4.2% alcohol, and one that seems to be on the rise, Bud Select, with 55 calories but only 2.4% alcohol.

Light beer tastes horrible; if I wanted to watch my weight, I would eat right and exercise. Something most Americans think they can get away without, by drinking light beer or diet soft drinks.

At least in America drinking your beer faster is encouraged; just look at the designs on some of these cans. The Miller hole punch, the Coors valve. "Tippy Cup, King's Cup, let's-get-fucked-up." I get it – to avoid the taste and low alcohol content, consumption must be increased. I guess it's lucky that it *is* low calorie, otherwise you would get fat before you got drunk.

Where I come from, when we crack a beer, we raise it to the bloke next to us, we drink it, and we spin a yarn. Women don't really drink beer in Australia; maybe that is why our women are skinnier than those in America?

To make matters worse, Fosters – "Australian for beer," has become a standard American stereotype of Aussies. The commercial has a put-on Aussie accent that gives you that same feeling as when a Kiwi talks.

Not that I would drink Fosters anyway; I don't even think they sell it anymore in Aussie bottle-o's. I believe Fosters was just bought by SABMiller, so isn't Fosters "English for beer" now?

Only in America do domestic beers suck, and ruin the beer culture. Beer should be enjoyed with every sip, not endured as quickly as possible to make it bearable.

Beer pong makes drinking light beer bearable

# ADVERTISING IS A WEAKNESS

Living as a poor college student, there are certain choices one must make – let's call them preferences, not choices.

I went to Missouri to see my old teammates from Southeast Community College for Ben's 21st birthday. It seems like only two years ago I was buying Transformers for his birthday.

Ben, Woody and Miller still played basketball, and over the Chrissy break they got an allowance for food since the tuck shop was closed.

Here is where preferences come into play. Food, or beer? Of course, they chose beer.

Now to my preference; back in January when I moved into my flat, I had to make a choice – cable TV or Internet? I chose Internet. "Duh" (said in a stoner American accent).

So my life since January has been very advertisement-free; ironic since I have an advertising minor. We went out for Ben's birthday and even snuck him into the bar an hour early (the details of this night are best staying amongst the people who were there).

Sunday rolled around, at least, I think it was Sunday – it was a big Saturday, possibly even Friday, night. Miller, Ben and I were laying in the dorms watching movies on American TV – so with no swearing or boobs.

At first, I was excited to see adverts again, they did interest me now that it was a possible career path. Plus, I was kind of out of the loop on how the new Wendy's burger was supposed to taste better than their Baconator I couldn't finish on Thursday, or how it was customer appreciation month at Subway, but not at the Subway in the ghetto of Columbia, Missouri, where we were staying.

The adverts were horrible. Full of contradictory information and terrible humour that only the guys who made them ever laughed at. I guess there is big money in the advertising game, even if you suck at your job.

One ad was trying to show that they had the fastest 4G phones by having two guys tailgating and posting their experiences to Facebook. After they posted the photos or statuses, people with supposedly slower phones came up to them asking if they knew about 'such and such' they had just seen online, to which the first two replied, "well, duh." The problem with this ad was that it didn't really show the company having faster internet than its competitors because those guys were the ones posting the statuses. I think it would have been a better ad for the other companies, whose customers were seeing the posts just a few seconds after they were posted.

Those that pissed me off the most, though, were the ads for certain medicines that could save your life – if you happened to be one of the only six people in the world suffering from such an uncommon illness.

They spent around 9 seconds explaining the vague benefits, another 9 seconds of testimonials, followed by a minute of possible side effects, risks of death and numerous reasons why you shouldn't take it. Again, terrible advertising.

From the advertising books I had read, I thought America would live up to the hype that the authors of those books (Ogilvy and Sullivan) had created. It seems that only in America is a company's greatest weakness advertising to an audience with IQs in the low double digits.

# BOXING DAY

*Published in* The Wayne Stater *11/01/2012*

Christmas is a great time to bag that extra video game or jacket you can't be stuffed buying yourself. What's even better is Boxing Day, provided you don't have to work.

This day is for rocking that new jacket while assassinating people from rooftops in your new video game, or when you get rid of less than average gifts.

The origin of Boxing Day is that you're supposed to box up all your unwanted gifts and give them to the less fortunate.

However, in more recent times, it has become: "This shirt doesn't quite fit me. Rick has smaller muscles than me. I'll give it to him," or "I can't fit me head through this Obese Records jumper, so I'll swap it with Dropsy's."

It's a great day to get my mates drunk and ask them what Santa brought, while hopefully watching the Aussies smash the Pommies in cricket.

Which brings me to December 26 in America.

No special name, no special cricket or American equivalent game; just the next day in the calendar year.

I could give it a special name based on the events that transpire.

Let's call it Return Day, the day where you return all the gifts you didn't like to the store where they were purchased and receive cash or store credit back.

Basically just slapping in the face whoever went out of their way to buy you something. I experienced this firsthand walking into Scheels and seeing three open registers, followed by a line fit for an AC/DC concert for six registers that were just for returns. If the gifter paid cash for the gift, you got cash back. I believe that in the criminal world it's known as petty laundering.

It's the perfect way for a stoner to get what he wants from his family for Christmas: return all shirts and pants for cash to go buy choof with.

Because let's face it, a stoner doesn't need a new shirt to show off to his mates, when he's just sitting in his bongalow pulling cones, hidden from the world.

I, for one, do not think I have ever returned something that was a gift, if it wasn't broken or actually not compatible. For instance, buying me an Xbox game when I'm clearly a PS3 guy.

My only answer is to "see through the superficial glitter of this season and to discover behind it the child in the stable in Bethlehem." Well that's not actually my solution; the Pope said that, but I agree with the first eight words.

Only in America can Boxing Day, a day intended for the less fortunate, be turned into an excuse for greedy consumerism.

Boxing Day Returns
Photo credit: Erica Lundstrom

# NOTHING LIKE THE OUTBACK

*Published in* The Wayne Stater *28/03/2012 as a resturant review*

I am sitting in a hotel room along with a couple of other Aussies, when an ad for Outback Steakhouse comes on. The inconsistencies between the ad and the actual outback were amazing. For one, there was a man driving a four-wheel drive across beautiful yellow sand next to an ocean of what looked like fresh water.

The real outback... aka the Great Australian Fuck All. Kilometre after kilometre of hot, red desert sand with no water in sight.

The signature dish at Outback is apparently 'shrimp on the barbie.' First up, shrimp in Australia means "little weak person" and, going off the people I hang out with, we are not cannibals, so screw you Paul Hogan for selling out.

We decide it is definitely worth going to see what they think Aussie cuisine is. As we walk in we are virtually slapped in the face by the display of boomerangs and didgeridoos. We are seated and await the arrival of the waitress.

Without skipping a beat, we are greeted with "Good day I'm 'what's her face' and I'll be your server." Her poor attempt at an Aussie accent lands her somewhere closer to the inbred Pommy next door. We laugh at her and ask what she recommends. She suggests kookaburra wings. I can't let that slide.

"You mean to tell me that you imported a protected Australian bird, killed it, fried it the good old fashioned American way, and are now trying to palm it off as a respectable dish?" She looks shocked and explains she tries to make everything sound more Australian to get better tips.

I let it go and continue to look over the menu – not a parma in sight. Can't be an Aussie restaurant and not have chicken parma, or fish and chips, or anything lamb for that matter. I want an entree (to Americans, entree is the main dish) or as the menu reads, Aussie-tizers. First thing that catches my attention is 'Aussie Cheese Fries.' What on earth is Aussie Cheese Fries? If it's not hot chips covered in vinegar or smothered in gravy then it is a lie (it turned out to be French fries topped with melted Monterey Jack, Cheddar, chopped bacon and spicy ranch dressing).

Other notable items on the menu are: Walkabout soup, salads with more dressing than a fashion show, New Zealand lamb and Norwegian salmon. Everything was cooked on the barbie and just in case you haven't heard the stereotype before, they reinforce it 4, 5, 11 times. All their burgers come with pickles, and not one comes with beetroot; I guess the McOz has it wrong in that regard.

The only genuine Aussie feature this place has is that the toilets are labelled 'blokes' and 'sheilas' (which might even be spelt wrong). The other thing I notice is they use cherry tomatoes with everything, as if my dad was out the back cooking.

When we are about to bail, the waitress comes over one last time to say, "Cheers!" We laugh, and since we are supposed to feel like we are in the Outback, we do not leave her a single cent for a tip, because in Australia, you do not have to tip. She should have known that, and maybe it will be a lesson to her, to not take the piss with that fake accent.

Only in America do they reinforce stereotypes to the point of creating an inauthentic outback restaurant. If it were truly an outback experience it would serve kangaroo meat, chicken parmas and meat pies, and if they insist on boomerangs and didgeridoos they might as well serve witchetty grubs, too.

*On the next page is a letter to the editor written in response to this review.*

# Free Speech

*Published in* The Wayne Stater *04/04/2012*

Dear Editor,

This is in response to "Nothing like the Outback" by Alex Osborne.

I agree that dining at Outback Steakhouse is not an authentic "Australian" experience, but hey, it's an American franchise.

What do you expect, really?

Normally I enjoy reading his impressions of American society.

But what troubled me about this article was the way he nonchalantly talked about stiffing the waitress on her tip.

You were NOT in Australia, mate, and she depends on tips to make her living.

She had a fake accent?

It's possible the management requires employees to do stupid things like that on the off chance that it impresses the people who don't know any better.

(One little old lady to her friend: "Ooh, our waiter said 'G'day' and sounded JUST like Mick Dundee!")

So after consulting the Internet for an Australian slang dictionary let me put it this way.

The sheila that was serving you is a battler just trying to make a quid.

Not tipping her makes you a dipstick as mean as cat's piss, and about as useful as an ashtray on a motorbike.

Next time you have a complaint about a restaurant, take it up with the manager or send a letter to corporate headquarters; don't penalize the waiter or waitress who is just doing his/her job.

Sincerely,
Ronald R. Lofgren
Associate Professor of Music

# MIPS

I remember when I was 15-years-old, my and my mates parents started buying us alcohol. Back then, a slab would last me a month; six beers every Saturday night. These days, a slab lasts two days at most. I couldn't imagine growing up and being afraid to drink because of underage drinking laws.

In America, a police officer can arrest you and charge you with a Minor in Possession (MIP) for having drunk as little as one beer, if you are under the age of 21.

My first week at Southeast Community College was the first time I heard about this law. Picture this: Westy, Zeus, The Fridge and Milk (all from Melbourne) lived together in the dorms. One night, like most nights before the basketball season, they decided to drink. Westy had just gotten out of the shower and as it was the end of summer, he wasn't wearing shoes or a shirt (the point of this will come up later).

It had gotten to about midnight and the party was fair deep. There was a knock on the door, and, being ignorant of the consequences, Westy answered it. It was the head of housing; she informed him that she had called the police. They lived on the third storey and people started bailing right off the balcony. He thought they were crazy, but knowing what I know now, I bet he looked like the crazy one, standing next to the lady who had just called the jacks, with beer in hand and no shirt on.

The lady explained that the police would come and breathalise everyone and charge them with MIPs. He thought "bugger it;" if everyone else jumped off the third storey, he could also do it. Westy grabbed The-Centre-For-The-Girl's-Team and over they went; it was super easy with their height; they scaled down and took off into the night.

Westy suggested they just camp out by the outdoor basketball courts, however, apparently, for the severity of the crime they had committed, two buildings away just wasn't quite far enough. So barefoot and shirtless he ran through the cornfields to a wire fence, which he tried to hop over. To his shock and surprise, it was an electric fence. Both his hands and his hammy were touching the wire; it threw him back around two metres. He lay there and watched the girl crawl underneath the fence.

While Westy was busy getting his body scratched up, the police arrived at the dorm and breathalised everyone. They found Milk and Zeus in the closet; to convince them to come out, they pointed red dot tasers at them. Both were charged with MIPs.

Once everyone had found their way back to the flat, stories

were swapped. Rufio had climbed down the balconies, come back up the stairs and gotten into his bed. T-Pain had just pushed past the head of housing.

The Aussies were four 20-year-olds who had been drinking without consequence since they were 15 or 16 and drinking legally since they were 18.

Only in America can you go to war and serve your country at 18, but not come home and drink a beer.

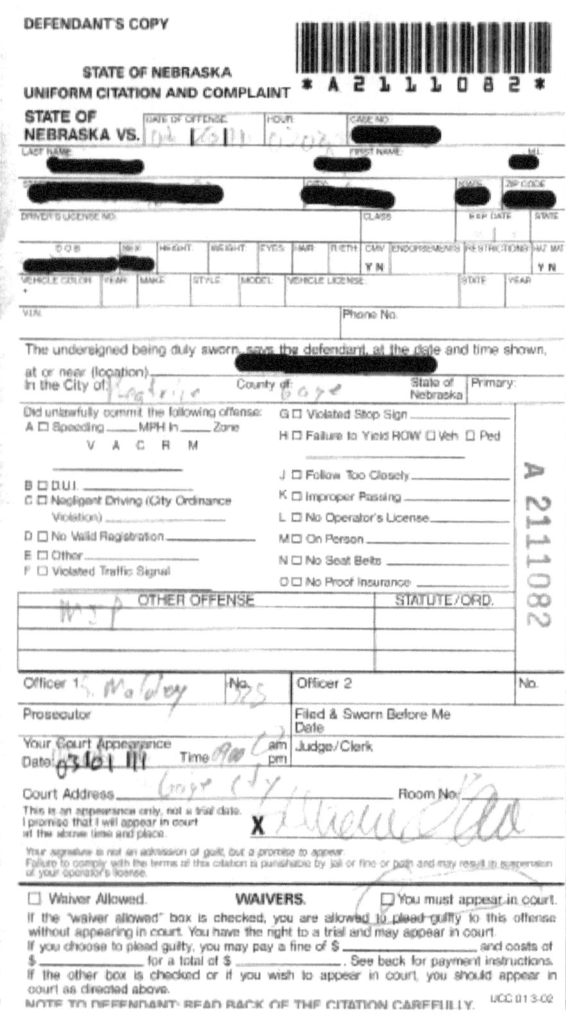

DEFENDANT'S COPY

STATE OF NEBRASKA
UNIFORM CITATION AND COMPLAINT

* A 2111082 *

STATE OF NEBRASKA VS.

Date of Offense | Hour | Case No.

Last Name | First Name | M.I.

Street | City | State | Zip Code

Driver's License No. | Class | Exp Date | State

DOB | Sex | Height | Weight | Eyes | Hair | R/Eth | CMV Y N | Endorsements | Restrictions | Haz Mat Y N

Vehicle Color | Year | Make | Style | Model | Vehicle License | State | Year

VIN | Phone No.

The undersigned being duly sworn, says the defendant, at the date and time shown, at or near (location)

In the City of | County of | State of Nebraska | Primary

Did unlawfully commit the following offense:

- A ☐ Speeding ___ MPH In ___ Zone
  V A C R M
- B ☐ D.U.I. ___
- C ☐ Negligent Driving (City Ordinance Violation) ___
- D ☐ No Valid Registration ___
- E ☐ Other ___
- F ☐ Violated Traffic Signal
- G ☐ Violated Stop Sign ___
- H ☐ Failure to Yield ROW ☐ Veh ☐ Ped
- J ☐ Follow Too Closely ___
- K ☐ Improper Passing ___
- L ☐ No Operator's License ___
- M ☐ On Person ___
- N ☐ No Seat Belts ___
- O ☐ No Proof Insurance ___

A 2111082

| OTHER OFFENSE | STATUTE/ORD. |
|---|---|
| MIP | |
| | |
| | |

Officer 1 | No. | Officer 2 | No.

Prosecutor | Filed & Sworn Before Me Date

Your Court Appearance Date: 03/01/11 Time 9:00 am/pm | Judge/Clerk

Court Address ___ Room No. ___

This is an appearance only, not a trial date. I promise that I will appear in court at the above time and place. X ___

Your signature is not an admission of guilt, but a promise to appear. Failure to comply with the terms of this citation is punishable by jail or fine or both and may result in suspension of your operator's license.

☐ Waiver Allowed. **WAIVERS.** ☐ You must appear in court.

If the "waiver allowed" box is checked, you are allowed to plead guilty to this offense without appearing in court. You have the right to a trial and may appear in court.

If you choose to plead guilty, you may pay a fine of $ ___ and costs of $ ___ for a total of $ ___. See back for payment instructions.

If the other box is checked or if you wish to appear in court, you should appear in court as directed above.

NOTE TO DEFENDANT: READ BACK OF THE CITATION CAREFULLY. UCC 01 3-02

MIP slip courtesy of a beautiful woman taken before her time.
R.I.P. darling.

# AMERICAN FOOTBALL: FOR THE LAZY

I sit down to write yet another column that probably won't make it into *The Wayne Stater* because I am writing with yet another hangover. Seems fitting since four Nebraskan cities just made the top twenty for the 'Most Hung-Over Cities' in the U.S.

Yesterday was the Capital One Bowl, the point of which I didn't really understand. It wasn't a championship or anything like that. It was just a football game with a massive cash payout to the winning school.

This bowl was between Nebraska and South Carolina. Not that Nebraskans need an excuse to drink their light beer in excess, but a Husker game is a major one.

The game started at noon, which is also when the drinking commenced. I can see why there are four very hung-over cities here, because watching Nebraskan football is a "win or lose, we booze" type of situation. If they win it's a good night; if they lose, the whole state gets depressed and domestic violence calls go up.

South Carolina won, of course. Nebraska only scored in the first quarter and that's when I stopped watching and just concentrated on drinking. American football is too slow a game to hold my attention.

These guys aren't really in shape, well, some of them might be, it's not like I am one to talk. I am just comparing American football to every other version of football in the world, and Australian football especially. Aussie footy players can run up to 15 km in a game.

A Yankee football player, however, might do a little pushing or sprint 40 yards per play, then get around one minute break between plays and upwards of 10 minutes while one team plays defence or offence.

Sport should be a two-way game. I used to play defender and goalkeeper in lacrosse. I was pretty good, too. If we were winning, I got to take a little break. I didn't get breaks for messing up like in American football. What I mean is, in American football, if I throw an interception or let my player get past me – guess what? Now the other team gets to come on and clean up my scraps and I have to sit on the sideline and rest.

I forget which game I was watching, as I was busy working on proving the stats for Omaha's 19.5 percent binge drinkers, but one team was penalised a few times for delaying the game. Yes, they actually think the game has a certain pace to uphold. Kind of like a shot-clock. There is enough time in this shot-clock to go to the kitchen, grab a beer, take a slash and come back before a play is picked.

Only in America is “football” more stoppage than startage and more rest than action. Or as Pulitzer Prize winner George Will has elegantly said, American football is “violence, interrupted by committee meetings.”

# THE METRIC SYSTEM

One of the reasons I became a journalist was to avoid maths and science classes. But as we all know, bloody gen-eds get in the way of that plan.

This past American summer, I took my third and final maths class, 'Topics and Ideas.' It sounded to me like we would just learn about what topics there are in maths and not actually have to learn them. I was wrong. Very wrong. SPOILER ALERT! I actually got an A in the class, but before that glorious day, I had a little frustration when learning the metric system.

I know what you're thinking: how does anyone, apart from Americans, struggle with the metric system? Well, let me tell you, this was no metric system I had ever used before. When the teacher mentioned we would be covering the topic, I thought, "you beauty, give me the test now and I'll rock it like Sam Worrell rocks Fridays."

My professor carried on teaching the class that 10 millimetres (metre spelt 'meter,' which my spell check is also trying to change) makes a centimetre and 100cm makes a metre and 1000m makes a kilometre – you know, the basic metric system that a lot of the world uses.

However, she then went on to inform me that here in America, they also teach that 10cm makes a decimeter, 10m makes a dekametre and 1mm equals 1000 micrometres. While the whole class was busy taking note, I delicately mentioned that I have been using the metric system for 22 years and I have never heard such bullshit before. I told her the metric system was supposed to be simple and you didn't tell people, "it's about 1 dekametre away"; you said, "it's about 10 metres away." If we wanted a difficult measurement system, we would have stayed with the imperial.

For argument's sake I will stay with length measurements to show the impracticality of the imperial system. Inches are the smallest unit of measurement. There are 2.5cm in an inch, 12 inches in a foot, 3 feet in a yard and 5,280 feet in a mile. What the fuck? If my house was a quarter of a mile from your house and I was trying to tell you how far away it was, I could say: "My house is about 400m away," but with the imperial system, I would have to either say a quarter of a mile or 1,320 feet away.

There is no logic behind it, and yeah, it is probably too late to do anything about it. At least when they teach the metric system though, they could teach it as a practical system, rather than making it complicated.

Only in America does the metric system become almost as unfathomable as their ridiculous imperial system.

# GOD IN NEBRASKA

If you have bothered to read my previous columns (and not just mine, but those of other *Stater* writers) you will have noticed that we went through a period of religion-themed columns. Some were tasteful, some were slanderous and others just took the piss.

Well, maybe I was the only one who took the piss. I had no idea the level of influence this God had over Nebraska.

When I played basketball, we did a lot of driving around the state for games and when we left during daylight hours and not at 5 a.m., I was able to take in the sights. It was almost like someone had painted over the windows of the van, because mile after mile was the same snow-covered landscape.

The only differences came in billboard form. As an advertising minor, I take notice of billboards. The only difference between these country billboards and billboards in the city is what is being advertised, and it's not a farmer-versus-suit type of situation.

I'd guess around 70 percent are about God. It never mentions whose god, so we can only assume it's the Christian God. Of these Christian billboards, the majority are about abortion.

Some of them have such slogans as: "Take my hand not my life," "Abortion kills," "It's a baby, not a choice," and "What if 'what's his face' was aborted," and in place of 'what's his face' they have pictures of beloved people like Lil' Wayne, Glen Beck, Rush Limbaugh and other men who think they can change the world with lies and deceit.

And you know what? These billboards have a lasting affect.

A couple of friends of mine have had experiences with the abortion 'culture,' for lack of a better word. One of them had to set up an appointment with security guards to escort her to and from the clinic, to protect her from the protestors' aggressive campaign. For instance, in Lincoln, Nebraska, anti-abortion groups throw eggs at women leaving clinics, unaware of the irony of their choice of aborted chicken fetuses for missiles.

Another mate of mine fell pregnant before she was married and without one having been requested, she told the father, "Abortion is off the table, because I am a Christian." Ignoring the obvious irony here, one possible the reason she said this was the guilt those anti-abortion campaigns will bestow on her, due to where she lives.

I don't understand how God can be advertised. I was watching tele the other day and I saw an ad that was actually *for* God. It was just a 30 second clip of people who look like muggers and people with road rage who magically receive lots of little pink love hearts from the sky that make their days better and completely transform their lives.

The ad is called "God's Love" and was created by the Interstate Batteries owner. Just a ploy for attention I'd say. I looked it up on the website given at the end of the ad and found an interview with this bloke. Wouldn't you know it? One of his main reasons for creating this ad was to stop mums killing their babies.

Only in America is God commercialised.

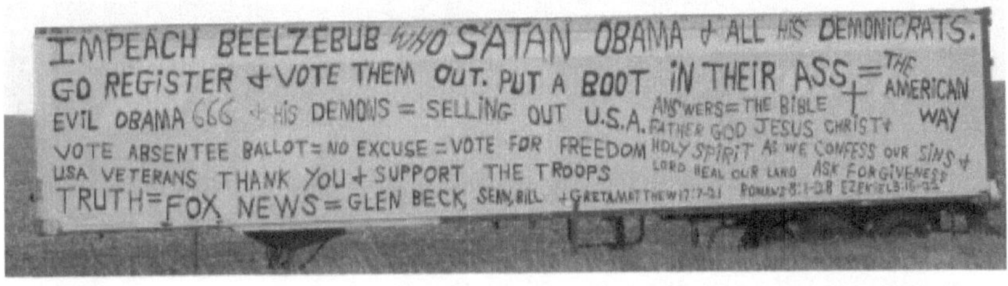

Homemade billboards in northeast Nebraska on Highway 20

# TOILETS

There are two things I do a lot of here in America. Number 1 is #2 and Number 2 is #1, I'll give you a couple seconds to have that one splash.

In case you're at a loss, I am talking about poos and wees. So I need to have a good dunny and American loos just frustrate me.

The reason I am going to the toilet so much is because of my diet. I now get free refills at Macca's, so instead of drinking just one medium (an Aussie large) Dr. Pepper, I am drinking two or three. Not to forget that dollar menu either, now instead of eating one McChicken, I am eating two or three.

First up, I'll start with taking a slash. I am yet to find a toilet that enables me to piss on the porcelain, so I am constantly having it splash all over the floor and seat.

The design of the toilets is the problem; the seat is low to the ground and the bowl is full of water. What I grew up sitting on, and standing in front of, was a higher seat with only about a litre or so of water in the bottom.

I don't think the lack of water in the bowls has anything to do with the drought we faced in Australia. I think it's because it's practical.

Second up is the poos; I am going to keep details here to a minimum to save you thinking TMI (too much information, for you gen-x folks). There is a big difference in the size, shape and colour of my stools here in America.

But back to the toilets. The American toilet design has a smaller bowl at the bottom of the normal bowl, that is located directly below the exit – creating cartoon-like pyramids that lead to me clogging or nearly clogging the toilet once a week.

In Australia, the bowl is on a slope with a large pipe to allow what exits to exit in the proper fashion. Back home I can't even think of a time where I clogged the toilet. Except for when I shoved a whole toilet roll in there.

Only in America, home of the massive turds, are the toilets designed to clog, and splash your piss.

# THE GREATEST SPORT IS CONSIDERED A FANTASY

If you didn't know, which you probably didn't, last Friday night was the AFL (Australian Football League) Grand Final. And no, I am not talking about rugby or soccer, I am talking about our own unique sport. Which I can't be bothered to explain, so look it up.

So I was in the *Stater* office trying to get people amped up for the big match, when one of the copy editors and writer of 'Marky Mark's Music Reviews' (I am sorry, mate, but I have to call you out on this) compared it to Quidditch.

"Quidditch? As in, Harry Potter Quidditch?" I replied.

"Yes, 'cause everyone is flying around," he said.

I laughed, a little excessively, and got straight on the phone to my old Aussie teammates from Southeast Community College, who also got a good laugh out of it.

This made me think about my first reaction to American football. Taking the piss out of gridiron seems to be a recurring topic for me. I would have to say at first I didn't understand gridiron; Mark didn't understand Aussie Rules, either. But, just like in AFL, the best part of the game is when someone gets cleaned up in a bump or tackle. So naturally I took a liking to NFL. Even going so far as to go out and buy Madden (I think it was '04) just to learn the basics of the game, enough so I could understand the one game of gridiron we got on Aussie TV, the Super Bowl.

I played Madden a lot at home; I thought I was pretty good at it, too. That was until I came to community college. In my first game I got my rear end handed to me by 70-odd points by a kid from Georgia. Apparently, knowing the rules helps.

As the year went on, I watched more and more American football, finding holes in the game and realising just how seriously people take their football (especially Nebraska fans).

One of the weak spots is the use of pads. Australian players don't wear pads, and they get hit just as hard and sometimes harder than the Yanks.

To get back to Mark's remarks (which, by the way, would be a killer column title for him) he was referring to the 'specki' aspect of the game. 'Specki' is short for 'spectacular,' which is exactly what it is. And what it is, is when one player jumps onto the back of another player in order to mark the ball. In American football, this is called passing interference and incurs a penalty.

Instead of having a spectacular catch for a touchdown, they decide to just settle for a simple uncontested catching of the ball.

Only in America is the greatest sport considered a fantasy by people who play a very unspectacular game, and who are afraid to take a bump without helmets and pads.

A Husker's football game

# CURFEWS

The stroke of midnight; that limbo time when you can't decide between late night or early morning. None of that matters to a 16-year-old kid. Because by this time of night, most parents are in bed and most young adults are hitting their drunken peak elsewhere.

It's that time of night where pinching a stop sign is plausible and the streetlights dictate victims to the next car prank or badging.

When you're staying at Jonny's, but he is staying at yours, but you're both actually staying at Bill's because his parents sleep upstairs.

In the park, where innocence is celebrated during the day, innocence is lost at night.

More hoses are stolen than cars, because you can't make a bong out of a car.

After midnight a cop makes you paranoid and will never make you feel safe. If a cop spots you, running becomes instinct.

To many teenagers, growing up in that nighttime pot plant is a necessity, it seeds out all of the petty crime early on. Teenagers don't like rules; you can tell them all day nothing good happens after midnight, but not one of them will believe you until they see it.

Back when I was a teenager, I would more often than not walk home with the crew at any time between midnight and 5 a.m., but no later than that, because I didn't want to meet my folks in an awkward coming-home-while-they-leave-for-work type of situation.

And believe me mate – we saw it all on those walks.

The craziest after-hours stories you have, we can top. They made us who we are today. Avoiding getting bashed or caught up in a police chase became second nature.

So it surprised me to hear that some states around America, Pennsylvania and Missouri to name a couple, have imposed a curfew on teenagers being allowed outside after certain hours.

In Philadelphia, residents younger than 13 have to be home by 10 p.m., while those under 18 can be out until midnight. Nobody under 18 can be downtown on Fridays and Saturdays after 9 p.m., with fines of $300 and $500 and parents held responsible for any crimes committed by their kids.

These curfews are to deter what they call "flash mobs," which I laughed at when I heard because all that came to mind was people who assemble in public to perform basically pointless dances or acts for a little bit, then bugger off.

But apparently a flash mob in Philly is described as consisting "only" of young black men organising themselves through social media to commit attacks, not to entertain the drones minding their own business.

Now, I've heard of calling a spade a spade, but I think there is a bigger issue here that a curfew will not solve, and one that I'm not touching.

Curfews do not solve anything. I had a curfew during school nights, it was to be home before *The Simpsons*, or watch *The Simpsons* wherever I was, then come home.

Can you guess what I learnt from this?

In the episode of *The Simpsons* when Chief Wiggum declares a curfew for the kids, who are being blamed for school vandalism committed by a drunken Homer and his friends, the kids fight back. The parents end up regretting their decision to impose a curfew.

I was one of the lucky ones, whose curfew involved watching *The Simpsons* and being home for dinner. Telling a teenager they can't walk home from a mate's house will only backfire.

Only in America is setting a curfew making your city more dangerous.

# DOUBLE DOWN

A couple years ago, I drunkenly entered a McDonald's contest to name the "Name It Burger." I came third and won free McDonald's for a year. This started me off making my own burgers when I went to Macca's as I got tired of the regular menu. I would order 'pounders' and 'quadruple McChickens,' and everything had to have Big Mac Sauce. Whenever I ate these things my face would drip with oil and I would get the itis.

My thirst for a grease-soaked pillow at night couldn't be satisfied, then one day Kayne turned me onto double Zingers at KFC. I had never tasted anything so good and we ate one every pay-day for a couple of months. That was, until it became too far away to travel by foot; something was happening to us. To put it bluntly, we were getting fat and lazy.

In my second year of uni, KFC in Nebraska trialed a new burger, the Double Down. The ad led me to believe it was a burger with two chicken breasts, cheese and bacon. "Oright!" I thought and I went down the street to get one.

I walked inside and placed my order; my mouth was watering. As I opened my see-through packaging, it came to my surprise that there was no bun. The two chicken breasts *were* the bun for the bacon and cheese. I struggled to get through it. My hands were dripping with grease, making it difficult to pick up my drink for some sweet Dr. Pepper relief.

This was just the start of the heart-stopping burgers I found in America. Wendy's was always a crowd favourite after basketball games – Quadruple Baconators, the name said it all. Burger, bacon, sauce, repeated four times. Delicious! Today however, these burgers stop me in my tracks and make my left arm tingle a little bit.

Now, I haven't tried this next burger. I have only looked at it and voted against it. The burger changed my mind so drastically that just looking at it made me want to drop to the floor and do sit-ups. It is the Krispy Kreme Burger. Glazed doughnuts as buns; you can't help but feel ill at the sight of it.

I understand the fascination with eating things that clog your heart – I was guilty of it when I was younger. What I don't understand is how grown-ups can eat these things like they are broccoli. A Baconator-a-day probably gives you diabetes and makes your sweat turn into cooking oil.

We have all seen *The Simpsons* episode where Homer tries to gain weight to claim disability. Well, I think Americans took this too literally: "Instead of making sandwiches with bread, use pop tarts. Instead of chewing gum, chew bacon." And the classic line, which should be the number one indictor you're going to get fat from eating this, "If you're not sure about something, rub it against a piece of paper. If the paper turns clear, it's your window to weight gain."

Only in America can *The Simpsons* give such clear warnings about weight gain and have them backfire and come out as encouragement.

# THE REALITY TV OBSESSION

In my first advertising class we spent the majority of our time watching *Mad Men* and looking at the latest Groupon. However, at some point, we actually had to do some work. We were asked to find the latest social phenomenon and create a product to tap into that market.

At this point in life, it was "a Jersey Shore thing." My idea was a hat that had a TV screen that flips down. 24/7 reality TV, also known as... reality.

One night my missus and her girlfriends wanted to have a *Jersey Shore* night to celebrate the start of a brand new season. I was invited, but I very impolitely declined.

Why is reality TV so popular?

When I watch TV, it is to escape from reality. Just kick back and watch pure golden scripted comedy, not bullshit, I-think-I-am-the-best-in-the-world drama from a bunch of ulehs.

My dream job would be to write for shows similar to *Always Sunny in Philadelphia* or *Modern Family*. If it were to be reality, it would be drawn real stories like *The Ricky Gervais Show.*

Back to *Jersey Shore*. In the years prior to this show (and I am going to generalise here) "guidos," or as they are referred to in Melbourne, "wogs," "ulehs" or "muzzas" already walked around like they owned the joint. Now, post-*Jersey Shore*, muzzas are walking around looking more and more metrosexual than ever.

Where I am from, if you want a tan, you go outside. And acting staunch only gets you extra knocked-out by real men.

Side bar: I Internet searched "guido" (using Google as a verb in print is illegal) and the Urban Dictionary's top result read "a sad pathetic excuse for a male; not necessarily of Italian descent, but most likely; usually native to the New York/New Jersey Tri-State area." I then Googled (hehe) "muzza" and found a very funny, very detailed description that I can't repeat.

*Jersey Shore* was just the tipping point for me. For years, *Big Brother* and its ilk, which the general public get way too involved in, have annoyed me.

It makes no sense to me as I have an IQ, but one of my professors explained that people who get caught up in television fall victim to "mediated personification" – the idea that you engage in de-individuation, which is the lack of self-awareness. We do this when we are in large groups, like in a sports stadium and we act as a group not as individuals. We also do it when we watch TV. We lose sight of the idea that the characters are fictional and give them life-like qualities. We then lose self-awareness and develop strong emotional ties to the characters.

I wish I could wrap this up with something clever about 'only in America' and *Jersey Shore*, but unfortunately it has spread to Australia.

# ROCK 'N' ROLL

I was sitting at Matt's the other night watching the college football national championship bowl. The only one of the bowls that was for something other than money and bragging rights.

A little bragging rights of my own here: in the national championship game there were two Australians, one on each team. I don't know how many there are in all of college football, but we have one on each of the best teams in the country – that's telling you something.

The game was boring, extremely boring. No big hits, no sweet touchdowns – in fact, there was only one touchdown the whole game. We spent most of our time trying to solve these little wooden puzzles Matt had. Once the fun from those wore out, Matt jumped on the laptop to look for a new cymbal for his drum set.

He found a pretty good looking one that had what looked like Arabic writing on it. Being as it was Matt's house and I was surrounded by three farmers, I decided to make a wisecrack I thought they might appreciate.

"You shouldn't buy that one," I said. "You should buy *'merican.*"

Matt went on to explain that he couldn't buy American, because America has outsourced almost everything, and even if they hadn't, America doesn't have the bronze to make good cymbals.

I came up with another wisecrack which this time I kept to myself – only in America do they outsource rock 'n' roll.

Which I found to be a true statement the next night when I was in Matt's pub. All of these small-town bars that I frequent have jukeboxes, and all of them have an ample AC/DC collection. Most nights when I'm out, I hear plenty Acca Dacca, which is fan-bloody-tastic. I have travelled halfway around the world and am hearing more Aussie rock than I hear in our own pubs.

More wisecracks from yours truly as I turned to one of the locals and said – "our best rock 'n' roll band."

He looked at me dumbfounded (a lot like the look I am told I give when I am asked a dumb question) and replied, "What do you mean, 'yours'? AC/DC is American."

As a gifted and frequent mass debater, I was determined to prove him wrong. We argued for two or three beers, we asked other locals and got nowhere. It wasn't until Matt came in with his smartphone and kindly looked it up for me that I tasted the sweet climax of victory.

America has outsourced everything to the point that they don't even know they are doing it anymore. Rock 'n' roll originated in the United States, but AC/DC holds down their jukeboxes.

Only the Americans.

Jukebox from The Greenhorn
Photo credit: Matt Richardson

# THERE IS ALWAYS A WIND

Thankfully, this past winter in Nebraska has been quite mild. Colder than I like it, but not as cold as it could be. One day it was in the high 50s (15°C), which is a nice, balmy Nebraskan day.

My mum sent me a text message saying, "It's snowing in Melbourne. 13°C overnight." Either she has divine powers to predict the future, or it was just a harmless joke with severe coincidental results – as the next day in Nebraska it snowed.

As many of you know, I hate the snow. I hate everything that comes with snow: the icy ground, fewer people in the bars, getting sick from going from super-cold outside to way-too-warm inside, but most of all, I hate the bloody wind.

The winter wind in Nebraska is too much to bear. I stepped outside my house in an attempt to walk the ten or eleven blocks to school. Even with the protection of my pants, skivvy, jumper, jacket, beanie and scarf, one step outside was enough for that piercing wind to penetrate through.

I had no idea how I was going to make it to school – I had to resort to desperate measures. I stuck my thumb out and off to school I attempted. You won't often hear this atheist man thank God, but thank God someone stopped. I was only two streets into the suicidal task of walking in the wind when a nice bloke named Brady (coaching and PE major) offered me a ride. And I got to school with plenty of time for the over-achieving girl in my class to remind me of the homework that I swear the professor never assigned.

In true journalistic fashion, I pumped it out last minute and went back to daydreaming and complaining to myself about the wind.

At least that day it looked horrible outside; I could have predicted the wind. The same can't be said for other days. Living underground doesn't help when it comes to predicting the weather outside and my trusty Swackett app has been letting me down in the "what-to-wear-today" department.

I used to have a weed that grew from my window-well, so I could tell when the wind was blowing. However, the old couple from above took it upon themselves to do a little weed-whacking and now all I can see is the sky. The Nebraskan sky is very misleading.

In Melbourne if the sun is out, usually I can bring the guns out, too – not true here. That wind, that wind indeed, that bloody wind, comes out of nowhere and ruins what could otherwise have been a lovely day.

I thought Nebraska was so windy because, as I had been told,

Colorado blows and Iowa sucks. I found out later there is a more scientific reason. The wind gets tunnelled through Nebraska as cold air comes from Canada, and the Rockies funnel it through the great flat states to the east of them.

Writing this outside today could have been an option; the sun was shining. But, as you can probably guess, the wind prohibited it. This column could have been about something entirely different.

Only in America does the sun being out not entitle a man to bring his guns out, for fear of being blown away.

# FRUIT AND BEER

Nice warm weather – perfect for eating fruit and drinking beer. Notice that those are two separate tasks: you have your eating of the fruit and your drinking of the beer.

What about mixing them together?

The result could be a delicious mix, a fruity beer. Perhaps a Leinenkugel? Leinenkugals taste like Fruit Loops; a pretty refreshing beer, especially on a hot day.

One day at the White Dog Pub, they had Boulevard on special. I am too much of a broke college student to turn down a special on beer. The bartender brought me a beer that had a lemon hanging off the top of it. I looked at her and reminded her I ordered a beer and not a fruity cocktail. She explained that you put the lemon in the beer. I did not like this idea.

The next day I was at Mikey's Pub and its special was red beer. After last night I wasn't going to risk it, even after the constant nudging from a girl I was seeing. I decided to just try hers – it's half beer, half tomato juice, stirred with a stick of beef jerky and a pickle.

Pardon my French, but that is fucking yuck. I refused to take even one sip.

I know I sound like I drink every night, but the next night, we had Blue Moons. Delicious! Now one of my favourite beers. However, this night I was with a mate who said we had to go to Pac-N-Save to get oranges. Oranges, I thought, I could go for a little vitamin C.

I didn't realise once again that the fruit goes in the beer – it isn't two separate tasks. I tried this one, a Blue Moon with an orange stuck down the neck. You know what, I kind of dug it, but I didn't feel like I was drinking a real beer.

I like "real" beer, and "real" beer doesn't contain fruit.

When I was growing up, the only beer we put fruit in was Corona. The only reason I put the lemon or lime in my Corona neck was because my cousin Matt told me that the lemon was to sanitise the bottle from the rat piss, from the rats that were in the shipping containers when the beer was imported from Mexico.

I believed him for years, until I came to America and saw that all the beers with fruit in them were American made.

So why fruit in the beer in America?

I don't get it. Maybe these American men are just one fruity beer away from just drinking cocktails every time they go to the bar. Like that *How I Met Your Mother* episode, when Marshall loves the gay club because he can drink fruity drinks without being ridiculed.

Only in America do they add fruit to beer to hide the fact that they would rather be drinking cocktails. If you like cocktails, drink cocktails, but don't try to hide it in your beer.

Drinking a Boulevard with lemon wedges

# DON'T WE BOTH SPEAK ENGLISH?

By now you're either sick of hearing about Matt the news editor, or you wish these columns were written by him because he sounds a hell of a lot more interesting. I don't blame you for either option. Unfortunately, this story starts off with his inspiration as well.

Matt and I have this language barrier: he thought he spoke English and I thought I did, too – but apparently not.

Our difference in language isn't a 'Matt and I' problem; it is an 'American and I' problem, or most likely, just an 'I' problem.

When I first came out to America to tour up and down the east coast, I kept running into questions about "who I root for." Being a single man with less-than-average looks, I told them I root whatever I can get. They looked confused, and rightly so.

I then flipped the question on to them – maybe this was some sort of American way of finding out whether one was in a relationship or not. However, the answers resembled a mass orgy, one that I wasn't too keen on getting involved in.

"I root for the Miami Heat!" she said.

"The whole team?" I replied.

"Yep!" she smiled back.

As I sat there in disbelief at how this 17-year-old girl was having sex with an entire professional basketball team, my coach, a seasoned American traveller, explained that in America, 'root' means 'barrack' and not 'fuck.'

That wasn't even the most embarrassing mix-up.

I was sitting in my maths class between two pretty attractive women and I was making small talk, while I did my work in pencil.

Maths is hard and a big reason I studied journalism. Naturally, I was making quite a few mistakes. I turned to the girl next to me – who at this point was buying into my whole 'hot foreigner' persona – and I asked her for a rubber.

She acknowledged me with a confused look and a nervous reply of, "umm… What?"

"A rubber," I said. "I just want to rub something out real quick." I made the hand gesture and all.

The girl's confused look turned to something of a scowl as she muttered something under her breath, I imagine now it was a harsher word for 'creep,' and packed up her books and moved to the front row.

Unaware as to what had just happened, I turned to the girl on my other side to look for answers. Before I could open my mouth she stopped me and said, "I don't have a condom, if that's what you're looking for?"

Now I was the confused and nervous one. I laughed and explained I didn't need a condom – "unless we gon' do it" – I needed an eraser to erase the mistake I made in my adding-up.

We both laughed pretty loudly in the back of the classroom. The girl in the front was still giving me the greezy of the year.

Only in America can the slight changes in lingo turn us all into perverts.

# LOVE THY NEIGHBOUR

I didn't want to do this, but these last 24 hours have left me no choice. First of all, on this week's entertainment page I made a harmless joke, saying that "if you think seven years of bad luck is too much for breaking a mirror… try breaking a condom." It is kind of funny, just a little joke to get you through class, and, unfortunately, kind of appropriate for college-age students.

Not everyone found it comical. A Christian organization on campus called Campus Crusades or "CRU," did not. That's completely fine. However, from CRU's dislike of the joke, stemmed a dislike of me. I feel obliged to share one of their Facebook statuses exactly as it was posted.

> "really Wayne Stater? One of your top statuses is from a UNL student (I think most people assume you are using statuses from Wayne State students – since that would make sense); your poll of the week looks good, but only 13 people voted, so that's less than reliable; Beer Brands Word Find? reallly classy/appropriate (NOT); why does that Australian guy try to be funny in every Stater? I guarantee less than 5% of readers find him funny or even interesting; Skinnys is the sketchiest place on earth (I speak from experience). [this status is very Dave Parrish-esque (whose article I actually enjoyed)]"

Let me take this apart statement by statement.

1. Complaining about the top status being from a University of Lincoln student: well solving that problem is simple. The entertainment page takes submissions – if you want Wayne-related statuses, then submit Wayne-related statuses.

2. Poll of the week: I am glad she likes the poll, however complaining only 13 people voted (which, by the way, is incorrect, there were 16) is once again her fault because it's a poll that is on Facebook. If the poll is inaccurate, then how did she even pull together her stat about readers not finding me funny?

3. Beer Brands Word Find not being appropriate for college students: I guess she didn't know that four Nebraskan cities are in the top twenty for most hung-over cities in the U.S. and are all college towns. I think it was very appropriate given those stats. And who uses 'not' jokes – talk about funny... Not!

4. Calling me not funny. You know what, she is probably right there, I never once said I was "funny or even interesting." If, as she guarantees, less than 5 percent of people like me, then I must be doing something wrong. Let's see if I can work on getting that down to around 1 percent.

5. The Skinny's article was written so my date and I could laugh about our night out. It might not have been the best place to do a restaurant review, but if you read the article, it is about a night of drinking and adventure – not of fine dining.

6. Dave Parrish's articles are stiff and boring, like he is.

To be honest, strict Christians are not really my target demographic.

The next day I was in my Communication Ethics class. Three Christians led the class discussion on how the Ten Commandments are a good reference point for ethics. That's a fair point; I am not against them in that regard. It was the way they handled themselves at the front of the classroom that pissed me off.

I was raised to make my own decisions. If I had wanted to follow the Bible I could have; if I had wanted to shave off my afro and become a monk, that was my choice. I was also raised to accept all people and to love my neighbour.

So when these Christians were at the front denouncing other religions and atheism, it kind of fired me up.

One of them said it was not a coincidence that everyone believes murder is unethical: it is because it is part of the Ten Commandments. Therefore every religion in the world that believes murder is wrong, and holds a different view on God, is wrong because it was the Christian God who told everyone not to murder.

It seems to me that historically other religions are less likely to murder people than the Christians.

Take the Crusades, for example: these were a series of wars sanctioned and blessed by the Pope. Is it coincidental that the Campus Crusades share the Crusade name, and are denouncing other religions in a classroom environment? A classroom in a state college, too. America's First Amendment says there must be a separation between state and church. It is supposed to protect me from being harassed about my religious beliefs. No government religion; in other words, the freedom to choose whatever religion I like.

A more up to date example – *The Boondock Saints*. This movie is about killing in the name of God (it's a bloody good movie). It raises these questions throughout and shows people being interviewed on their thoughts on killing in the name of God.

Only in America can they preach the Ten Commandments as the basis for ethical decisions, while at the same time breaking "Love Thy Neighbour," by not loving me, their neighbour, and my freedom to disagree.

# TV CENSORSHIP

There are a few reasons why I don't have cable TV in America. The first is because of my Couch Theory (the idea that sitting on a couch with a girl in front of a TV leads to a realtionship with her), the second is cost-related, and the third is because of the 'muckalucking' silences and 'fruiting' changes to the best lines in movies. Changes due to swearing or because they contain words not suitable for 10-year-olds. To make matters worse, there isn't even a fair compromise, like more tits – or even any tits at all.

Just recently the FCC has been copping some scrutiny for allowing 'profanity' (their term, not mine) on cable TV, but not on free-to-air. The argument they use is something along the lines of: kid's programming is on specific channels on cable but is among the mix on free-to-air. The other reason is obvious – you pay for cable.

I, however, disagree with their arguments. I have watched cable TV during my time here in America, and profanity is nowhere to be found. Except on HBO, but Americans say that there is TV and then there's HBO. Meaning that it's an anomaly.

But why should HBO be the anomaly? I watched HBO to find out what kind of programming they had on. I found *Summer Heights High*, an Australian show, which probably needs a little swearing so Jonah is funny. Another program I found was *Flight of the Concords*, a Kiwi show. One chick I slept with told me she learnt how to give gobbies off of programs on HBO.

So maybe it's a culture thing. Down in our neck of the woods, swearing and tits are tolerated on TV. But it's not like Americans don't swear – some of the best comedy movies are American.

You can imagine my frustration when trying to watch *Superbad*, where just about every dialogue scene had something silenced or changed. *Superbad* uses the F word 176 times. What is the point of showing this movie if someone has to sit there and change the F word into something else, or bleep it out 176 times?

The same goes for radio: why bother playing those songs where for the best bits, I'm sitting in silence while the bloke next to me says the line and butchers it?

What happened to freedom of speech? We let TV become privately owned when it is one of the most public forums. Only in America is your First Amendment right only guaranteed as long as someone else does not own you.

# BURT REYNOLDS - BETTER THAN A SUPER BOWL

*Published in* The Wayne Stater *08/02/2012*

Sunday is that one night of the week where it is vital you do homework instead of drinking White Dog Super Mugs.

However, last week, Sunday was designated a party night.

Being a foreigner, I forgot that. I usually put off all my homework until Sunday night; I use the rest of my weekend for hittin' the piss. Depending on when I get done – Super Mugs, here I come.

As a journalism major, I usually have one story a week to write, another Sunday task. This week, I had three; two of them are columns, so it wasn't too bad.

It is funny that "less than 5 percent of readers find me funny or even interesting" yet I hold down over 5 percent of the paper.

Now it is a beautiful Monday morning, and I am awake early typing my articles, while a cat tries to fight my Ugg boots.

So what on earth did I do yesterday?

Most of you wasted your Sunday drinking Budweiser and eating Doritos while watching the Super Bowl, because that's what America has come to expect of you.

They know that you will be watching, but more importantly, they know you care about the commercials.

Last week, we all hopped online and took a little sneak peak of what ads were to come.

Lo and behold, Budweiser and Doritos headed it up once again. So that is what you bought as munchies on this past foggy Sunday.

I, on the other hand, slept right through the first half – I might have enjoyed my Saturday a little too much.

The second half, and the rest of the night, I spent watching Burt Reynolds movies – *White Lightning*, *Shark, Gator* and even an episode of *Archer* that he was in. *Smokey and the Bandit* is on the download list ('download' has a negative connotation, so let's say 'rent online' instead).

Say what you will about these movies, but fair dinkum if he ain't the Harry Potter of gun-running and moonshining.

Burt Reynolds says watching his movies are "more fun than going to an all-night dentist."

The opening scenes are what gets you pumped up for a little Burt.

All three movies have a very similar plot, and the two movies where he plays Gator McKlusky are almost exactly the same.

In all three, he gets laid in or next to water, and there is some form of sweet car or boat stunt, a fat cop who dies and a blonde love interest.

*White Lightning,* though, has the most elaborate prison escape.

It is this kind of thinking that has Gator above other franchise actors. Gator doesn't even consider anything difficult, he just runs right up to the fence and hops over it.

"My films are the kind they only show in prisons and in airplanes, because nobody can leave," Reynolds has also said.

I guess my weekend hangover was my airborne prison, because I was not leaving.

Only in America is the Super Bowl so American and commercialised that one must spend that time otherwise, by watching Burt Reynolds.

And just like Burt, there are only two things in the world I'm scared of, "women and the police."

# THIS IS NARNIA

*Published in* The Wayne Stater *29/02/2012*

After waking up from a DayQuil nightmare of six dead bodies under my bed and sex with those uleh girls from my high school (I knew those souvlakis would catch up with them) at the late hour of 1 p.m., I see my roommate and his mate just sitting there, looking out the window at the sunny Saturday that could be. With no work and no play, make something, something happen.

Wayne, America: the suitcase college town. A bloody nightmare for a boarder left alone on the weekend.

But there is a magical wardrobe with a mystical land just outside – Wayne's very own version of Narnia. But this Narnia comes with semi-automatic weapons, a Green Diamond, and less incest and Christianity.

Adventuring through this wardrobe isn't as simple as just stepping through.

One must buy beer and $10 sunnies and drive to northern Nebraska with enough weaponry to take down tweakers and immigration alike.

The lamppost in this Narnia is a two-foot fire on the edge of the Missouri River, fuelled by floorboards and satellite dishes. The fire will keep its creators warm when the White Witch shows up with her ice and her snow.

We were more interested in following the fawns, trying to shoot them with our semi-automatic weapons. Something had spooked them; they were high-tailing it out of the southern cornfields and into the forests of the north.

We arrived at the cabin; it had been empty too long and the Asian bugs had taken control.

Our targets had already been laid out.

The duct-taped .22 missed and splashed snow across the yellow circles, but the AR-15 made light work of the reds, exploding them onto the compact snow beneath.

The first friendly casualty of the day came when we were driving up Rattlesnake Road. A mixture of ice and mud made one-armed steering difficult.

The Colorado slid from one side to the other, avoiding the banks like it kept its money under the mattress. Halfway up the snake's back, the road became too much, and the driver's second hand was forced onto the wheel, spilling beer into his lap (I know what you're thinking Max, but this was Narnia – different rules apply).

On top of the snake, we found the Green Diamond bar and

paused to regroup.

George Washington's face lined the walls of this bunker, but not even he knew what day it was. At least he would have agreed with the guns, and been glad that this was still America.

As day turned into night, we headed back to the regular world.

We made one last stop for some food and chatted to the women who had dreamcatchers in their bellybuttons.

I like mine swallowed.

Back in Wayne, we stepped into the smoky cigar haze of acoustic guitars, bass, big-boy vocals and a harmonica that kept the devil at bay.

And as the music played, that morphine feeling pulled at my cheekbones.

Only in America? Or was this Narnia? Or, maybe, just another Dayquil nightmare?

# YOUTUBE IS KILLING THE MUSIC INDUSTRY

*Published in* The Wayne Stater *21/03/2012*

"You see, the problem with music these days, is YouTube," he says. "Everybody is a star nowadays, a wannabe, you know?"

"Like we are, when we sit here and write things that no one will ever read. We are just trying to be the next big thing, in a world that doesn't care about us, right? 'Cause we are nobody."

"Yeah mate, 'that shit cray.'"

"I don't even know what that means."

"No one knows what it means, but it's provocative."

"What the hell are you talking about?"

"Some terrible, 'thinks it's music', rap song. The way I see it, everybody jumped on that Justin Bieber bandwagon, and people with sensible music taste are still paying for it to this day."

"But I liked Justin Bieber before he was famous."

"Congratulations mate, you were underground. But now, you're Hollywood. You sold out, or, more likely, you're just playing Simon Says with the DJ of KFRX and Channel 94.1, and underground is cool – at least, that's what Hipster Weekly said."

Whatever happened to rocking a live set for random people? What happened to the love of the music? The pride?

What happened to writing a song and taking a risk in front of a crowd of people who have the option to walk away?

If they click on your YouTube video and hate it, you still get the view, so you can't gauge anything.

Most importantly, what happened to hip-hop?

This isn't going to turn into a column about the state of the hip-hop game, because most of you are content with this Hollywood hip-hop, rapped by blokes who have made their fortune and are now spending their questionable talent telling you that they are richer than you.

Yes, you, the same you who supported them and made them rich. Bloody shame on ya. Get your lazy arse off YouTube and watch some live music.

This past Saturday was St. Patty's Day (as if you didn't know), and live music was more than available. There were so many live shows in the surrounding Wayne area that you couldn't possibly have seen them all.

I made the decision to go to Wisner with a couple of mates to see the Cactus Flats.

These guys are among the select few in this day and age still living and rocking the live music scene.

They are top blokes and invited us onto their tour bus for an Old Milwaukee before the show.

At the end of the night we were across the street listening to The Back Forty, because they rock a mean show, too.

If only DJ Smith's show wasn't in Laurel. He is a one-man wrecking crew and I would have liked to have seen him.

Live music is where it's at, fellas.

Get off YouTube and support someone who is making a real effort, like Vito Cole. And Sean Badeer; if Vincible has a gig before I go home, I would love to check it out.

Only in America am I famous in *The Wayne Stater*, but with nobody reading my stuff because I am a nobody. Just another wannabe trying to get famous so I can write about how famous I am, and then neglect the people who got me there.

*On the next page is a letter to the editor written in response to this column.*

•

# Free Speech

*Published in* The Wayne Stater *28/03/2012*

## Dear Editor,

This letter is in response to last week's article on the same topic.

That article asserted that YouTube was negative for the music industry, and was essentially a place for people to put music out there to hide and get views and not be criticized.

I agree that people need to go to live performances. This is the purest form of music, and the one that most directly supports musicians. When you buy a CD or MP3, you'd be amazed at how little of your money goes to the artist.

When you go to a live show, it's a much higher percentage. What I find issue with in that article is…well, everything else.

First, the contributions YouTube has made to the music industry are undeniable. For a very large example, I point to the band Journey.

When they were in need of a new lead singer, they turned to a YouTuber who posted videos of himself singing Journey covers, and right now, he's on stage somewhere with the band as its new star.

YouTube is a place you can go try out a band, or find unknowns. Never heard of Cage The Elephant and aren't sure if you want to fork over $20 for the band's CD?

Head to YouTube and you can listen to almost any of their songs.

Sure, YouTube has its low points like Fred and Justin Bieber, but anything that contributes to Journey is alright with me.

Sincerely,
Dave Parrish

# SOBRIETY CAN KILL

*Published in* The Wayne Stater *26/04/2012*

G'day, my name is Alex, and I have been sober now for three days and my god am I bored.

It has come to my attention this past weekend, after spending more than enough time at the Nebraska Collegiate Media Association, that the classic image of a journalist isn't the sitting-in-the-bar-after-work-drunk type, but more the straight-laced-judgmental-sober type.

I skipped out on the majority of conferences and talks and went for a walk to find someone either as hungover as me or someone who wanted to grab a midday drink; failing that I would have settled for someone who was just as bored as I was.

I found one person who shared my opinion of sobriety, and how it might actually kill us if we were to abide by it. We were the only people still up at 5 a.m. partying.

The majority of the day I spent by myself, except when I went and bought a pool with Kayla and Travis. After that I took a nap in the sunshine, and then walked around the campus avoiding the judgment of others for the entertaining lifestyle I chose to lead.

How do you think the entertainment page is created when no one submits anything?

I lead an entertaining life.

A lot of you who know me, know by now that I like to drink and you usually blame it on me being an Australian.

Yes, Australians like to drink. It isn't criminalized by any means like it is here. No underage drinking law, the ability to buy alcohol at 18 years of age, and the freedom to not be judged for drinking during the day, or before or during important events.

Ever wondered why the Foster's can is so large? It's because it was originally created by VB as 'a lunch beer.' As in, a beer you drink on your lunch break.

So to those who judge me for having a few drinks here and there, remember – a glass of wine a day keeps the doctor away.

And since this is my last column for *The Stater,* I will take this opportunity to conform to the judgmental American society.

Next time any of you feel like judging someone who isn't from here, you should take a closer look at your own backyard and reconsider.

The First Amendment says there shall be no state religion and that you have the freedom to practice whatever religion you see fit.

So throwing a Bible at the foreigner, who is only abiding by this American law, is breaking the Founding Fathers' laws.

For those who have taken in Jesus and feel the need to save me on a daily basis, let me put this to you.

If the Christian God exists, which he doesn't, then hell exists. And if hell exists, then you're a fool to think that we aren't already there.

I realise I am already there, and you judgmental people are Satan's minions who dish out torture to the people down here.

Instead of torturing everyone; drink a beer or two and calm down.

Not everybody who has read the Bible has gone on to become a good bloke.

Hitler was a Christian, and you are just a couple of judgments away from your own holocaust.

Take calm in knowing this is the last you will hear from "The Australian."

I have enjoyed abusing your freedom of speech and freedom of the press while I have been here.

It is funny that nothing I have said can change what goes on in this country. But that's the society they have imposed upon you.

So go ahead and continue to wear pads during your so-called football games, hide behind your guns when someone lips off, prosecute people for drinking, and continue to judge the world while not realising what the world thinks of America.

This is your America and that's fine, I'll be gone soon.

If you want to talk further, I will be drinking at the White Dog, or drinking in my pool.

I'll shout you a beer if you come… but a real beer, not a light beer.

Only in America can sobriety kill you.

# Guest Columns

The following guest columns were contributed by family and friends of mine from Australia and England, who have also spent some time here in America and have their own stories to share.

**Adrienne Osborne**
Relation: Mother
Nationality: Australian
Came to America for work and twice to visit me.

**David Synnott**
Relation: Next-door neighbour in Wayne, America
Nationality: English
Moved to America at 14 to play baseball.

**Jessica Meisels**
Relation: High school mate
Nationality: Australian
Came to America to study.

# BOTTOMLESS DRINKS

Adrienne Osborne

They say meal sizes in America are huge. I knew to expect that, but what surprised me was that Americans are well-watered, too. Coming from a country that had just struggled through 14 years of drought, I watched in amazement.

They say, "When in Rome, do what the Romans do," so at my first restaurant, I cheated a little and ordered water instead of a soft drink. All around me people drank from these huge glasses filled with soft drinks. They had to have at least half a litre in them (I later found out there is 473 mL in a small Macca's drink). When the glasses were about two thirds empty, they were exchanged for full ones. The customers drank (and ate) on. I couldn't keep up. I couldn't even drink all of my one glass. Maybe that's because I didn't eat the pickles.

It made me wonder what the queue was like to the toilet.

Speaking of the toilet, you nearly sit in the water to pass those bottomless glasses away, the toilet bowl is so full. Water, water everywhere – I am waterlogged!

If people drank less soft drink, would the levels of water in the toilets need to be reduced? How could people think or function without their constant sugar highs? How many associated industries would go out of business? It boggles my mind. Maybe I need a sugar high to stop worrying.

There is a shortage of soft drink in Australia at the moment. We'll survive. Only in America though, would such a shortage bring a nation to its knees.

# DRIVE-THRU LIFESTYLE

David Synnott

America – the land where there is never enough time in the day. The place where you always have something to do or someone to please. Where I'm from, England, people are busy, too, but they take time out of their day to sit down, have a cup of tea and catch up on the news or with their family. A night out with the family in England might be a two or three hour trip to the supermarket to get the shopping done. America – not so much.

No matter where you live in the world, you can experience the classic drive-thru window at McDonald's or Burger King, where the food is supposedly fast *and* fresh. Lines back up into the parking lot and orders are messed up, so you end up having to go inside anyway, which defeats the object of the drive-thru in the first place. I agree that sometimes, when you are in a rush or on a road trip, the drive-thru window is the best option. But does it really take that much time and effort to go inside to sit down and eat?

You can still bring your smartphone in with you so friends will know what you are doing, since it is a must that everyone knows you are "eating a mcdouble #myheartheartsgrease." Well apparently eating at fast food restaurants is not the only place where Americans don't want to make the effort to go inside and spend more of their precious time. How about drive-thru pharmacies, coffee kiosks, kwik shops, and much more. The ones that really crack me up are drive-thru banks and drive-thru liquor stores.

Now where I'm from, there is no such thing as a drive-thru bank. The idea of having to roll down your window and tell a microphone what you want to do with your accounts and your money is obscene to me. I don't know about you, but I like to keep my financial transactions as private as possible. Why would I want to yell my account numbers out so other customers or passers-by can hear them? The word 'fraud' comes to mind.

Who knows what pieces of technology could be hooked up to those mics, especially in this day and age. I feel that your money, and how you handle your money, warrants you a 10-20 minute trip into the bank; besides, the bank usually provides you with a nice treat like a biscuit or a lollipop.

Now for the pièce de résistance, a drive-thru liquor store. This just amazes me. I know this doesn't mean that every driver that uses these stores is drinking while they are driving, but why tempt them. The driver is obviously not going to get out of his or her car to put the alcohol in the back or in the trunk, otherwise there is no point in using the drive-thru. So the driver has to put it somewhere in reach of where they are sitting. This should not even be an option, especially in a country where drunk driving is responsible for "39 percent of all casualties."

Instead of spending tax dollars on ever increasing DUI checkpoints, wouldn't it be easier to just outlaw drive-thru liquor stores or even make it illegal to have alcohol in the front half of the vehicle? Not only will the government be saving time and money, but they could also be saving lives.

I understand that people are busy and trying to make the most of their time, but are they really making the most of their time by rushing through things? Sounds clichéd, but sometimes taking 10 minutes out of your day to do the small things is what life is truly about. You know, like writing a paper and people-watching with a cup of coffee.

Drive-thru bank in Wayne, Nebraska

# COFFEE IS A DESSERT

Jessica Meisels

Let me explain. Whilst travelling through the great U.S. of A, I found myself at many a Starbucks counter, asking for drinks I learnt were part of a cultish "secret menu" (which really means 'go to our website and click on various ads to find out about our latest drink'). But whenever it got to choosing what "style" of milk I wanted, shit got real.

In Australia, it is simple – you either want full cream milk, skim milk (likened perhaps to America's 2 percent) or soy milk. That… is it. No complicated variations. Milk means milk. In America, I was asked if I wanted cream, half and half, 2 percent, soy, fresh from the cow's udder, with a dash of Harvey etc. Until I just went ahead and said cream, figuring it is their way of just saying, you know, 'milk.'

It isn't.

I was devastated. Finally, I thought, a coffee that didn't taste like dirt mixed with Charlie Sheen's tiger blood. Finally, a drink I could have alongside my healthy serve of fried and crumbed fruits and vegetables. Astoundingly, 15 pounds, yellowed teeth and a questionable amount of sporadic energy later, it turns out that 'cream' is actually *cream*. Yes, yes, cream comes from milk blah blah, but it isn't the same.

According to trusted source Wikipedia, cream is "a dairy product that is composed of the higher-butterfat layer skimmed from the top of milk before homogenisation." This means anywhere from 18-30 percent of your coffee is fat, and that's before you've wolfed down your morning waffles and unkosher bacon.

What I want to know is, do they even realise (sorry, realize) what is happening? What are the Olsen twins drinking on the 'got milk' ads?

For the love of God will someone just tell me where I can get milk that tastes like real milk?

*This column was contributed by Jessica Meisels, who now adds a scoop of ice cream (low fat) to every coffee.*

# TRAFFIC LIGHTS ARE RACIST

Jessica Meisels

I'd never seen anything like it before. Everyone (bar the colour-blind) knows the rules. Green means go, red means stop. But in America, it is a whole different ballgame.

I geared myself up at a traffic crossing and waited for the little green figure to appear and send me on my way. Normally, in Australia, I wait for the beeps to let me know when it is time to go, but as Alex touched on, America hates the blind, so there is no sound. I looked up when the figurine changed and was horrified. It wasn't green, the universal symbol for go. It was, or is – white – how racist? How is everyone else supposed to cross the road? Dodge traffic like they are at a Thai 'suggested' crossing point, whilst the white people skip along safely? Swim? Hoverboard? Swing from a makeshift rope? Drive everywhere, even across the road? I swear, if I had a nickel for every time an ethnic person stood next to me at an American crossing and went "Oh, man, not again!" and stormed off – I would still be a poor arts student. But you get my drift.

It's funny, because their Civil War-era pedestrian crossings are in stark contrast to their coffee. Where asking for it 'black' or 'white' is equivocal to saying Oprah isn't that great, or Michelle Obama's arms are average (learnt that the hard way).

I say it is time for a complete overhaul of the American pedestrian crossing system. It's 2012, and according to the U.S. Constitution we are all created equal, and therefore everyone should be allowed to cross the road, no matter what colour they are.

Green works – it is meant to be therapeutically calming, is it nature, it is all of us. We get it. Minorities of America unite, and let them know that you will not be cannon-balling from one end of the street to the next any more!

*By Jessica Meisels, a female who just realised that it is a little green man. Shit, where's that cannon?*

# Final Thoughts

# HELL OF A RIDE

This is the end of the ride for "Only in America." It is a sad day when the dream ends and you have to hang up your boots.

I came to Wayne State College with no dreams or expectations other than finishing school and retreating back to the warmth and comfort of Melbourne's streets and 11:30 p.m. adventures.

I have done it all: from basketball, to being the engaged-foreign-kid who could only hang out until 10 p.m. before the wife called, to becoming single and being whispered about every Wednesday when the paper came out.

Newspaper pimpin' ain't easy – let me be the first to say it. Most of our staff played it safe and did their job very well. I joined the staff as Assistant Sports Editor. I was like the scorer in a basketball game: the players (the 'actual' Sports Editor) did all the work; I was just there to let him know what the score was.

A horrible job, it was boring, and most of all, it was too safe. If I was going to waste my sober time in an office, in front of a computer, I needed to take pride in it.

That is where the entertainment page came in; I created my own job. There were mixed feelings about that page.

Soon after the introduction of the entertainment page, I became infamous around Wayne's campus and the surrounding community. I had students harass me over things I published about their friends. I had an entire Christian organization boycott my existence. A professor suggested, "shut it down and find a new honours project," after I took a quote from her out of context for our *Overheard* section. I also had a pair of students speak to a lawyer about me publishing a status relating to their bad break-up.

One of my favourite situations didn't actually result in a reprimand, and was a story I only told to a select few. A young couple took to heart a made-up missed connection directed at a generic image of a woman, believing it was about them. They broke up over it.

The worst incident, referred to as the "Public Relations Nightmare," came about after I published a 'Sexual Positions' word search in my final issue. With this, my entertainment page apparently crossed some invisible line set forth by the Wayne community and a few very outspoken (on the Internet) virgins (I'm guessing).

On a beautiful spring day, the head of College Relations for WSC found himself involved in a countywide outrage when he received numerous phone calls about the page. The *Stater,* however, received only one.

The complaints were related to the "vulgar" and "inappropriate" material found on the entertainment page. The word search was deemed inappropriate for the image of the school and the surrounding community who read the newspaper. In a Facebook apology made by our Editor in Chief, 155 multi-paragraph comments were posted discussing the issue and whether or not it had been appropriate.

My comments in my defence were overlooked. "The page takes submissions, and based on the pretty sexual submissions I received that week for our *Overheard* section, I deemed a sexual position word search appropriate for the people who like the page enough to submit content." However, the intellectuals of the campus and community were so deep into their argument amongst themselves that it became clear what this was all about.

It was about local businesses, professors, and the public relations department having a controversial, pseudo-intellectual conversation. One of the more outspoken professors, it turned out, taught ethics. I have taken an ethics class: it is a big debate class with no clear winner on either side, just animated discussion.

Although he never mentioned what he taught, it seemed that he was just on there promoting himself as an intellectual, and therefore, indirectly, his class. I also got the feeling the public relations director was using Facebook in order to avoid the legal proceedings that go with talking on the record.

The same week as the Public Relations Nightmare, my column *Sobriety Can Kill* was published. My boss at Chartwell's sat me down and called me a 'communist' after reading it to me word for word. I had a few blokes come up to me in the bar and try to fight me over it.

I have also received a lot of praise. The head of Public Relations for WSC called me a "genius" (prior to 'his' nightmare); some have added me on Facebook to sing my praises, most of the people who doubted me or yelled at me apologised in the end – I even kissed one of the girls who had a go at me.

I have met some of the best people here in Wayne: Mr. Chad M. Christensen, you saved me from homelessness and showed me the wisdom of the Couch Theory, you also sparked the writer in me. A pool doesn't make up for it, but it's a start. My *Stater* staff, I love you all despite our obvious lifestyle differences, cheers for putting up with me. The Englishman, thanks for contributing, it was nice to have someone around who understands the filth that comes out of my mouth. I won't forget your wise words, Big Slim The Farmer. The three pretty blondes, you know who you are. And to the woman who has my heart – I apologise, you deserved the best.

I wouldn't be anywhere, however, without my Southeast Community College brothers; I would never have settled into America without you muppets: Miller, I will never forget your 21st and I am honoured to be Z's godfather. Salinas, you probably contributed a lot to my behaviour that first year as you bought most of my alcohol, and remember, "all cows are black in the dark," mate. See you again for some one-on-one beer pong. The young'un Benny Boy, you were our child prodigy, seeing you dominate on the court and kiss women brings me no greater pleasure as your mentor. We held it down for Australia, and never let anyone outdrink or outmuscle us.

Erica – I love you with all 200 of my centimetres, and I will definitely see you when I am 30 for that steak dinner.

And one more thank you to my beautiful editor Kacey, I can't thank you enough for the hours you have spent editing this mess. Hopefully 'Murphry's Law' is wrong.

Now I have graduated and am entering into the big bad world of grown-up journalism, where I will probably have to write about how well our government is doing, and how Joe and Mary Blow just had their 60th wedding anniversary. Instead of doing the fun and 'entertaining' stuff I have been privileged enough to be allowed to do – even if the majority of the time I was just takin' the piss.

I have been loved and hated, sought-after and despised, but most of all, I've been down for the adventure and experience. It has been one hell of a ride.

Only in America can you have this much fun.

# Glossary

*As requested by the WSC Editing for Publication class.*

**Acca Dacca:** AC/DC
**AFL or Aussie Rules:** Australian Football League
**Aussie:** Short for Australian
**Balmy:** Nice and warm
**Barrack:** To cheer or root for a team, as in "I barrack for the Bulldogs"
**Billabong:** Pond
**Bin:** Trashcan
**Biscuit:** Cookie, both savoury and sweet
**Bloke:** A man
**Bongalow:** A bungalow in structure, used as a haven for smoking bongs
**Boomerang:** An Aboriginal tool, crescent in shape.
**Boot:** Trunk of a car
**Bottle-O:** Liquor store
**Bugger:** Aussie synonym for 'fuck'
**Choof:** Marijuana
**Chrissy:** Christmas
**Cooee:** To be within shouting distance
**Didgeridoos:** An Aboriginal musical instrument
**Dishy:** Someone who washes dishes for a living
**Doco:** Documentary
**Dropsy:** My mate's name (also a swelling disease)
**DUI:** Driving Under the Influence
**Dunny:** Toilet
**Esky:** A cooler
**Exercise:** Any bodily activity that enhances or maintains physical fitness and overall health and wellness
**Fair dinkum:** Far out or true
**Fark:** Alternative spelling for 'fuck'
**FCC:** Federal Communications Commission
**Flat:** Apartment
**Footy:** Football
**Fuckt:** Alternative spelling for 'fucked'
**G'Day:** Hello
**Gen-eds:** Genral education classes, a requirement for all students
**Gobbies:** Blowjobs or headjobs
**Greezy:** A dirty look given mostly by girls
**Guido:** Douchebags from Jersey Shore
**Hammy:** Hamstring

**Hittin' the piss:** Getting drunk
**Holden:** An Australian car company
**Hungry Jack's:** Burger King
**Itis:** The sleepy feeling you get after a large meal
**Jacks:** Police
**Jumper:** Sweatshirt or hoodie
**Kookaburra:** Australian bird
**Loos:** Toilets
**Macca's:** McDonald's
**Mark (verb):** Catching the ball in Australian football
**Meat pies:** Australian delicacy. Similar to a beef potpie, only way better
**MIP:** Minor In Possession
**Missus:** Girlfriend or wife
**Muzza:** A person from Italian or Greek descent who thinks they're hot shit
**Nebby:** A zine published by Pseudo Poseur Productions
**Oi:** A term used to get people's attention
**Parma:** Chicken parmigiana, the stock-standard is a crumbed chicken breast with ham, tomato and cheese on top, served with tomato sauce (ketchup)
**Pièce de résistance:** A French saying referring to the best part or feature of something
**Pinching:** Stealing
**Pint:** A larger sized beer that can be ordered at the bar
**Pommy:** Term for people from England
**Pot:** A small beer you can order at the bar
**Pot plant:** A potted plant
**Prawns:** Big shrimp
**PRIDE:** A gay and lesbian organization
**Root (verb):** To have sex with
**Rubber:** Eraser
**Runners:** Sneakers/trainers
**Scheels:** A big sporting goods store
**Shrimp:** In America, prawn. In Australia, a small or weak person
**Singlet:** Wife beater or tank top
**Skivvy:** Thermal shirt
**Slab:** 24-case of beer
**Slash:** To stand up and urinate
**Soft drink:** Pop, soda etc
**Specki:** A spectacular method of catching the ball in Australian football
**Spin a yarn:** Tell a story or talk shit
**Stubbies:** Bottled beer
**Take the piss:** To make fun of

**Thongs:** Flip flops
**Tiggy:** Tag
**Trackies:** Sweatpants
**Tuck Shop:** Canteen, cafeteria etc
**Uleh:** A person from Italian or Greek descent who thinks they're hot shit
**Uni:** Short for university
**Ute:** A pick-up truck
**VEISHA:** An annual celebration held at Iowa State University each spring, and one of its oldest traditions
**Winningest:** Best winning record for sports
**Witchetty Grubs:** An Australian insect, eaten by Aboriginies
**WOG:** Western Oriental Gentlemen. This has become a derogatory term
**WSC:** Wayne State College
**Yanks/Yankee:** Americans
**You Beauty:** Thank you or well done

www.ingramcontent.com/pod-product-compliance
Lightning Source LLC
Chambersburg PA
CBHW031327060726
47590CB00003B/1361
*9780989363617*